THE TROUBLES OF MAGNET BOY

AND OTHER GLOOMY TALES

WRITTEN BY TOM BURLEIGH

ILLUSTRATED BY KAY DAWSON

2nd print edition. May 2016.

Contents

Little Zombie Susan

Little Zombie Susan,
sitting in a tree,
R O T T,
I N G!

First came bugs,
then came flies,
then came a crow,
pecking at her eyes.

Maggots,
more flies,
a gaseous eruption.

Putrid,
necrotic,
fleshy
corruption.
Bloaty intestinal
walls eroding,
massively inflating,
and finally exploding!

KD

Marcus the Stalker

Another zombie: Marcus,
sat perched upon a higher branch,
(slowly being dissected
by a marching line of ants).

Sobbing uncontrollably,
he stared down from above,
at his one and only truly unrequited love.

He'd loved her since their childhood,
to him she was perfection.
He'd offered her his heart and soul,
she handed back rejection.

Though he should have been dissuaded,
his belief remained unshaken;
that he could win her over.
Alas he was mistaken!

For years he tried to woo her
with increasing desperation,
he became a slightly crazy
brooding social aberration.

Desire became obsession
and poor Alice grew afraid.
A strict restraining order failed
to dampen his crusade.

A court of law sent Marcus down
for three whole months in jail,
but Marcus, being Marcus,
was still sure he would prevail.

Awful news awaited him
the day they let him go:
Alice had moved and changed her name,
and hadn't let him know!

He soon resolved though
to forgive this huge betrayal,
and resolving he should let her know,
got straight on to her trail.

For months he studied tracking
and with all the things he learned,
he launched a tireless search for her,
leaving not one stone unturned.

He hacked the deed-poll register,
he talked to all her friends.
He bugged her parents' telephone,
and found her in the end.

Alice now was Susan,
and was living happily,
with her anxious past behind her
in a town beside the sea.

The anxiety all came flooding back
one bright and sunny day,
she spotted Marcus on the street,
turned and ran away.

In panic she ran out into
the road without due care,
she was hit by a car and flung quite far
through the salty seaside air.

Her injuries were awful
and her body couldn't cope.

But though she died

and Marcus cried,

he still didn't give up hope!

He launched back into research
and learnt all that he could
of the darker side of Voodoo,
of dolls and chicken blood.

He learnt an old dead language,
and finally he read
a truly ancient ritual designed to raise the dead.

One dark and gloomy evening
he went to Susan's grave,
he took some chalk and candles,
a goat,
    a knife,
        a spade.

He dug down to her coffin.
Around the grave he wrote.
He danced about and chanted.
He sacrificed the goat!

And lo! Behold the thunder
and lightning from above,
and Marcus standing graveside,
his face suffused with love.

A lightning bolt stabbed downwards,
the plywood coffin broke,
and Susan's rotting corpse reared up
and tore out Marcus' throat!

As he lay there dying
Marcus finally realized;
he was in fact: quite disliked,
perhaps even despised.

And soon, he was on
a downward spiral of decay.
And Susan, still aloof, denied
his corpse the time of day.

NO
DOGS

Introducing Dog Boy

Like a werewolf, he was bitten,
and when the full moon came,
his tiny little body underwent a massive change.

He wasn't bitten by a wolf,
he was bitten by a child;
a strange and naughty little girl,
undisciplined and wild.

Forever he was changed,
from his owner's pride and joy:
a small and yappy dog,
to a hairy almost boy.

The Amazing Antimagnetic Girl

I

Until she was twelve
she seemed very normal.
Her parents were loving,
if often quite formal.
They dreamt of a life for her
better than theirs,
and hoped to instil in her
Graces and Airs.
So they sent her to learn
at a prestigious school,
where girls became Ladies,
and life there was cruel.
(The school had a history,
steeped in tradition,
of snobbery, bullying,
and naked ambition).

At first she did well though,
she was pretty and smart,
she excelled in Music
and Cooking and Art.
She had taste in abundance
and followed the trends,
and soon she had an over-abundance of friends.
It didn't seem to matter
that her parents were poor,
her looks and her girliness
counted for more.

II

But as she grew, inevitably,
puberty came along,
and in her case it brought something
quite horribly wrong.
At first it wasn't noticeable,
but as the months progressed,
it put her popularity
and friendships to the test.

It started with a discovery
of a trick that she could do:
if she stared hard at her pen,
she could make it slightly move.

Delighting in this miracle,
she practiced hard and played,
and soon with concentration
she could make it fly away.

She next tried other objects,
like her ruler, (made of wood),
and the hamster in its cage,
(made of fur and flesh and blood).

She tried to push a table,
she tried to push a chair,
she tried to push a strand
of her own shiny long blonde hair.

Through experiments she found out
that her power was elemental,
and only worked on objects
made with ferrous types of metal.
And further it was limited
to pushing things away,
and bit-by-bit was growing
slightly stronger day-by-day.

III

In a matter of a few short months,
her happiness dissipated
with the onset of a symptom
she had not anticipated:
one day she simply could not grasp
her knife and fork at dinner,
and being civilized, that meant
she started getting thinner.

The field of force grew outwards,
and stopped her touching things,
like taps and pans and kitchen knives,
pins and guitar strings.

About this time her friends became
a cold and distant group,
of snobbish taunting bully-fiends,
who dropped her from their troupe.

Now it seemed important
that her parents were not rich,
they called her nasty nicknames,
like Pauper-girl and Witch

The teachers too avoided her
and acted hard and cruel.
They started work on paperwork
to throw her out of school.

They didn't understand themselves
just why they were so vile;
she was still smart and pretty
and she still had ample style.

But in spite of her looks and girliness,
despite her skills and talent;
their blood contained iron and so
they found her quite repellent!

IV

Outcast now and lonely
and receiving harsh abuse,
she became an angry bitter
temperamental sad recluse.

One night feeling frustrated,
she went to bed and prayed;
"Please God, give me wings,
so that I can fly away!"

That night she dreamt of flying
and awoke with a strange feeling.
She opened up her eyes and found
her nose pressed to the ceiling.

With some surprise she fell back down
and landed on her bed.
She dressed and raced into the grounds
with wild thoughts in her head.

She concentrated now upon
the earth's metallic core,
and lo! Behold she lifted gently up
from off the floor.

With thought and concentration
she controlled her high ascent,
and a wave of joyous levity
displaced her discontent.

She next tried moving sideways,
not expecting to succeed,
surprisingly it worked though...
she managed it with ease.
With satellites and airborne planes
to push off she could fly
in any direction she desired
throughout the crowded sky.

She looped-the-loop and spiralled high,
she dropped and soared and swooped,
and happier than she'd ever been,
she shrieked and laughed and whooped!

Looking down from far above,
she gave a goodbye wave,
to all her former friends below
and then, she flew away!

Rat Boy part one.

The Origins of Rat Boy

Rat Boy wasn't really
a hero at all,
and he certainly wasn't a boy!
In fact she was simply a rat I dressed up,
and played with like she was a toy.

I somewhat suspect
that she took them to heart,
those playtime delusions of mine,
for I've seen her flying
at night through the skies,
no doubt on his way to fight crime.

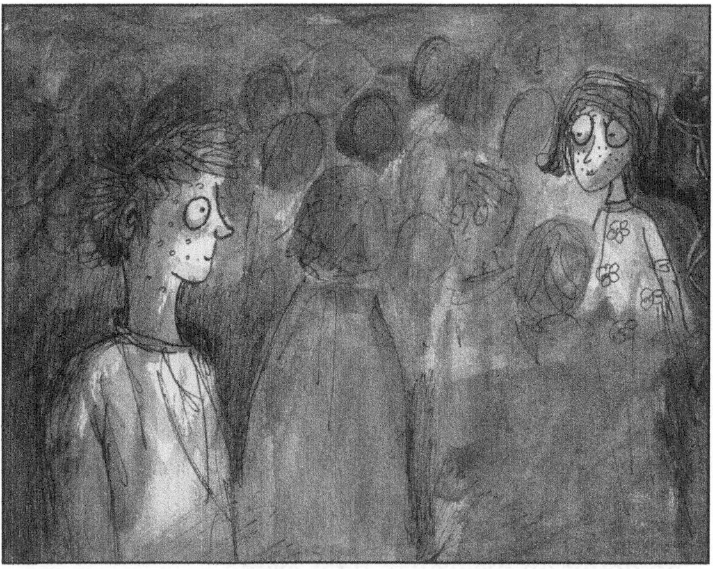

The Brief Sad Love Affair of Pimple Boy and Dimple Girl

The DJ put a record on,
a slow romantic tune;
and Pimple Boy saw Dimple Girl
across the crowded room.

Their eyes met and their hearts leapt
and their minds began to race,
with thoughts and words and images
of tender hot embrace.

In years to come they both laid claim
to true love at first sight;
among those dancing bodies
on that balmy summer night.

Neither of them moved though,
they were stuck fast in their places,
firmly rooted to the cheeks
of two young human faces.

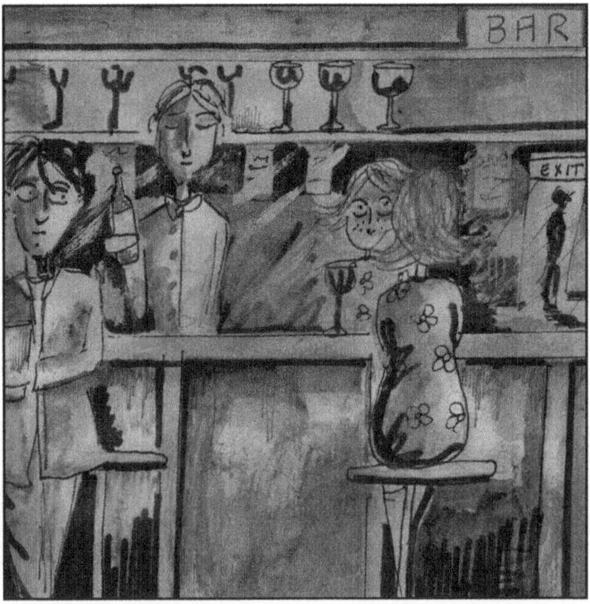

One human walked towards the bar,
the other to the door,
and Dimple Girl and Pimple Boy
were parted evermore.

Floristry

The Curiously Named Evil Doctor Strange

Working one evening
alone in his workshop,
his thoughts returned to his childhood.
Gently he picked
at the scabs of his mind,
and memories came back in a flood.

He remembered his parents,
stood sombre and sad,
with tears welling up in their eyes,
as they heard some more news
of his aberrant views,
his tricks and his traits and his lies.

By then he'd abandoned
the pointless attempts
at making his parents feel proud.
Their lives altogether
were fraught and frustrated,
with fractious and thunderous rows.

Now he stood at the worktop,
trying to remember
the last fateful terrible day,
the day they had thrown
him out of their home,
and said to him: *"Son, go away!"*

The whole thing was blurry,
the memories gone.
He decided he needed to know:
the cause or the reason
that finally freed him
to live as he wanted, and so:

He picked up the telephone,
dialled a number,
he held up the phone to his head.
The other end picked up
and a voice said *"Hello?"*
Then quickly and hoarsely he said:

"Mother, don't hang up!
Please answer one question.
Honesty please now,
no lies or deception:

What did I do
that so drove us apart?
Caused you such anguish
and shattered your heart?

Which made you so hate me,
and made things so hard,
that its been 20 years
without one Christmas card?

Without even one letter,
one miserable phone call!
No offer to meet me,
no contact at all!"

She paused before speaking,
planning her response.
When it came, it was dripping disdain.
Obviously still,
she was harbouring a grudge,
and still firmly held on to the pain.

She said: "*Son, you're a waste*
of a good education,
your ways cut us deep to the heart.
We were all so distressed,
even you must accept,
that our lives are much better apart.

We didn't much mind
your deceits and your lies...
your father and I taught you how.
And we must take some blame
for your complete lack of shame,
which you seem to have kept until now.

But it was hard on your father,
your refusal to join him
in the business he built up from the ground.
We might well have coped,
if you hadn't then chosen
a career path so awfully unsound.

The choices you made
are what hardened our hearts;
made us treat you like you are a stranger;
your desire to abide
by the laws of the land,
and your career AS A FLOWER ARRANGER!

Tell me what is so bad
about being a Mad Doctor?
An Assassin? A killer? A crook?
Your Dad - rest his soul -
was so good at his work
that they drew his exploits in a book!
Well... a comic, I admit,
but he'll live on forever!
And not just as a brain in a jar.
Oh he had such dreams,
and such devilish schemes,
and he always took things too far.

His camp villainy
was so thrilling to me,
and if only you'd been by his side,
as a team you'd have seen
the success of his scheme
and be ruling together worldwide.

But no, you with your morals,
your conscience and all
of those old sanctimonious rants.
Go now and stop whinging,
you sad disappointment,
get back to your flowers and plants!

Did I answer your question?
I don't really care!
You're a kill-joy and really no fun.
If I have my way,
you will scurry away now,
and NEVER let on I'm your mum!"

The curiously named
Evil Doctor Strange
gently put the phone back in its place.
Then he sank to the floor
with his head in his hands,
and tears flowing over his face.

Crayon

Rat Boy Part Two

Rat Boy Vs. ?

In the daytime Rat Boy
was a mild mannered Mother,
raising her young in a sewer.

At night he was a caped
superhero patrolling
the streets for the evil wrongdoer!

He believed that each Hero
had an equal and opposite
Crime Lord with whom he might war.
And he rather regarded
the commonest crimes
as a frightfully tiresome bore.

He ignored the drunk drivers,
the muggers and fighters,
the car thieves, the vandals and all,
and instead searched the night
for his Crime Lord to fight,
and deliver him to his downfall.

But the nights turned up empty,
all trails went cold.
Not one scrap of proof could be found,
that ever a Crime Lord
had organized crime
in the dark side of Rat Boy's town.

As each week passed fruitless,
his frustration grew;
little Rat Boy was fully aware
that it's rare for a rat
to live more than 2 years,
and to him this seemed awfully unfair!

For a rat of his powers,
his talent and prowess,
should be lauded and loved for all time!

But how could that happen
if he failed to find
even one Evil Master of Crime!?

The Boy Who Turned into a Boat

There once was a boy
who turned into a boat,
a small sixteen footer with sails.
His arms became mast
and his fingers the rope.
The rudder grew from his toenails.

This happened at night
and his parents, in fright,
were awoken by an almighty crash,
as a ceiling caved in
under pressure from him
and his lengthening, strengthening mast.

They called for the doctor,
they called for a priest,
they called out the Fire Brigade,
but no one could offer
a hope or a prayer
that their son, as a boy, could be saved.

HOLY
BIBLE

In the cold light of morning
they sombrely hoped
their offspring had suffered no pain.
Then they got on the telephone,
comparing prices,
and hired a truck and a crane.

They loaded him up,
with excitement they took him
to the sea where they set him afloat,
(they hadn't much liked
their son as a boy,
but they had always wanted a boat!)

Fluff Girl and the Dust Devil

Fluff Girl was an angel,
or so her parents said,
born from out of dust collected
underneath their bed.

They'd always wanted children
and welcomed her with love.
They viewed her as a gift divine
from Heaven up above.

Other kids were naughty,
Fluff Girl was good as gold,
she never threw a tantrum
and she did what she was told.

While other kids ate junk food,
her wildest food desire
didn't stretch a whole lot further than
the lint from the tumble drier.

In every way young Fluff Girl
seemed a parent's perfect child:
bright and quiet and healthy
with a temper calm and mild.

Coffee
Tea

She brought her parents happiness
and harmony in their home,
but in her private thoughts
and quiet moments on her own...
she dreamt of something different,
she craved a certain spark,
she projected wholesome goodness
but her inner heart was dark.

She longed for thrills and danger,
for wild and reckless nights,
for absolute abandon,
for drugs and drinks and fights.

When finally she came of age
and moved out on her own,
her dark desires like dormant fires
flared up to overflow.

ADMIT ONE

Dust Devil was a terror,
a whirlwind harsh and wild.
Abrasive and rapacious,
and often much reviled.

He ate up bugs and tumbleweeds
and dried up soil and dirt.
Those few who hung around with him
would often end up hurt.

But in his heart-of-hearts
he was a kind and loving soul,
and wanted most to meet someone
who'd make him feel whole.

Hot
FooD
served

They met one fateful starry night
at a dirty desert bar.
They talked and walked and later on
they stared up at the stars.

Their fingers touched,
their pulses raced,
they stood very close and face-to-face.

Lost in a moment,
in a state of bliss,
they leaned in for a magical
and tender first kiss.

And Fluff Girl was swept up
by the spiral of his wind,
and her fluff filled each
and every part of him.

Together they ascended
far up into the sky,
and together they exploded
with the soft sound of a sigh.

Then quietly and prettily
they fell down very slow,
on a lonely patch of desert,
like a blanket of fresh snow.

Dog Boy’s new job

Dog Boy liked his new job at the city’s cat shelter for the sense of despotic power it gave him.

Cod Boy

I

Cod Boy dreamt of the ocean.
He longed to swim wild and free.
If not for his parents' devotion,
he'd have run off to live in the sea.

They lived on a farm in the mountains,
a hundred miles and more,
from the comforting salty waters
of the seas beyond the shore.

His childhood days were troubled,
with rarely a smile or a laugh,
flapping forlornly in puddles,

sleeping at night in the bath.

His parents did all that they could do,
they really tried ever so hard.
They fed him and loved him and dug him
a large briny pond in the yard.

But as he grew older his parents
could see his unhappiness grow,
and they knew that the time was approaching,
when they'd have to let their son go.

Happy
birthday

II

On the day of his sixteenth birthday,
they drove to a town on the coast.
They bought him a raw seafood dinner
and his father proposed a toast.

He said “Here’s to my wonderful son,
our slippery wet bundle of joy!
Your Mum and I love you so much.
Happy Birthday, our dearest Cod Boy.

What I’ve got to say now isn’t easy,
and I’m doing my best not to cry.
The time has come, you must leave us,
and sadly we must say goodbye.

On land your uniqueness is weakness.
You’re more of a fish than a man!
We want you to live your life happy,
out there in the Ocean you can.”

III

They walked down the seafront together,
he entered the waters alone.
As the ocean enveloped him fully,
he finally felt he was home.

He swam with his soul feeling freedom,
he swam with his heart feeling joy,
his body instinctively moving,
Fish taking over from Boy.

IV

But he was… very slightly ungainly;
though more of a fish than a man,
he still had the limbs of a human.
As well as a tail, he had hands.

Compared with any other human
he swam with extraordinary grace,
but the cod were all natural born fishes,
and sadly he couldn't keep pace.

He languished behind feeling saddened,
hoping they'd welcome him in,
but cod lack compassion for stragglers
and they made no exception for him.

The Girl with Glowing Red Eyes

I

The sweet little girl
with glowing red eyes,
was taunted by boys
so she stayed home inside.

She played with her dolls,
and her small plastic oven,
imagining cakes
and pies by the dozen.

S P
EAT
your
5
A-DAY

II

The sweet Dinner Lady
with glowing red eyes,
was picked on and laughed at,
the subject of lies.

Lies about witchcraft
and demon possession.

Lies about deviant
sexual obsession.

They said she was evil,
malodorous and mad.

Those bad little boys
made the poor lady sad.

FAMOUS Pies
PIE 1
Pie

III

The happy old lady
with glowing red eyes,
has a very large oven
for baking her pies.
Her pies are now famous
in cities and towns.
They sell by the thousand,
all golden and brown.

The town that she lives in
is quiet... but has tales
of a surprisingly large number
of missing young males.

Yes, one day they'll catch her
and say: "*Her head isn't right!*",
but right now she's having
the time of her life!

The Life and Death of Poster Boy

I

Poster Boy was gorgeous,
a beautiful creature.
Graceful of poise,
and angelic of feature;
but lonely and fearful
and shy as a mouse,
he rarely got past the front door of his house.

He was so very pretty
that the people who saw him
were rarely contented
to stand back adoring.

They'd gather around him
and try out their chances,
with flirtatious talk,
and amorous advances.

Inevitably his beauty,
working much like a drug,
would make someone rush in
and give him a hug.

And a hug, even tender,
was terrible for him,
as he was so incredibly,
terribly thin!

II

He was home all-alone
on the evening he died,
he'd opened some windows
and wind got inside.

A freakish strong gust
caught him up like a kite,
and carried him out
and off into the night.

In the morning a girl
found his crumpled remains,
in a rain flooded gutter,
all soggy and stained.

She took him back home,
not disgusted at all;
cleaned him and pinned him
on her bedroom wall.

BREAKING NEWS....
WORLD
IS THIS THE END?

Antimagnetic Girl Saves the World

Part One

I

The news declared an asteroid
was on its way to Earth.
Science confirmed the size of it:
its length, its weight, its girth.

The bloody thing was massive,
and on its current course,
would hit the atmosphere with violent
cataclysmic force.

All attempts so far to change
its course had been in vain,
and the world would soon be heading
for a whole wide world of pain.

CAFE
TAXI
WORLD
IS THIS THE END?

Panic gripped the people
in the cities and the towns;
they ran and cried and tried to find
some safety underground.

They swapped their nice apartments
for sewer lines and caves.
In filth they hugged each other close
and prayed they would be saved.

II

All alone, in her woodland home,
Antimagnetic Girl didn't know,
she didn't have the Internet,
Television or Radio.

She now was 23 years old,
she'd lived alone for years,
she'd almost gotten used to it,
but still shed frequent tears.

III

The first she knew of the asteroid
was the shadow that it cast,
as it blotted out the Sun
approaching very, very fast.

She looked and saw an outline
growing larger every second,
a few minutes now from impact;
just one or two she reckoned.

She panicked for a moment,
then determined she would try
to stop the coming impact
and she shot into the sky.

At seven miles up she stopped
and hovered at that height,
she focused on the asteroid
and pushed with all her might.

With delight she sensed the innards
of the asteroid were dense
with iron and ferrous alloys,
and even though it was immense,
it quickly slowed its progress,
responding to her force,
and in the very nick of time
it faltered in its course.

Improbably it floated there,
a massive rock from space,
held in thrall to one small female
of the human race.

Controlling vast magnetic fields
and the iron and rock and dirt,
she flew five hundred miles south
to a sandy hot desert.

And there she gently laid it down,
and set off heading home,
back to her quiet forest life,
alive... and all alone.

IV

Around this time some science folk
realised they were not dead,
and set out to try to figure out
what had occurred instead.

They searched the skies with telescopes,
they checked their calculations,
they talked to all the astronauts
in orbiting space stations.

Soon they found the Meteorite,
and with satellites in space,
could clearly see the flying girl,
could almost see her face.

They tracked her to her woodland home,
and soon it was overrun
with media crews and scientists,
impressed with what she'd done.

TV

The Media wanted interviews,
the scientists wanted blood,
and permission to do some simple tests
and anything else they could.

Her power though was far too strong,
no one could get in close,
before they were repelled and felt
disgusted and morose.

Kept some 60 feet apart,
they questioned her with pages,
strapped to stones and flung across...
the interview took ages.

The news crews sent the story
beaming out across the world,
of how they'd all been saved
by Antimagnetic Girl.

Then the whole wide world rejoicing,
sent gifts from far and wide:
clothes and flowers and fluffy toys
and cards with cash inside.

And soon Antimagnetic Girl
was rich beyond belief,
and had more fluffy animal toys
than she had room to keep

Antimagnetic Girl Saves the World

Part Two

A journalist came forward
with a bad case of anaemia,
and a camera made of Bakelite,
which filmed in tones of sepia.

Her chronic iron deficiency
meant she could get in close,
and though she was a sickly girl
she still was quite verbose.

They talked first of the asteroid,
and then they talked for hours,
about her life and difficulties
living with her powers.

They talked about her family,
then they talked of her old friends,
they talked of global politics
and current fashion trends.

And finally the interviewer
became more personal;
she wanted to know everything
about our saviour girl.

She asked about her private hopes,
the dreams locked in her head,
her desires for love and romance;
Antimagnetic Girl said:

"Though I'm now famous,
and though I'm now rich,
I still have no Boyfriend,
I've never been kissed.

I've dreamt half my life
and I won't give up hope.
But if I don't get a boyfriend,
I'll struggle to cope.

Somewhere out in the world,
there has to be
a man with an opposite
polarity.
Who can touch me and kiss me
and cuddle me tight,
comforting me
through the dark woodland night.

Yes, somewhere out there,
there has to be
a magnetic man who is trying to find me!"

The Troubles of Magnet Boy

His magnetic pull
was so very strong,
that sadly poor Magnet Boy
didn't last long.

Rat Boy Part Three

Rat Boy Vs. Evil Doctor Strange

Rat Boy was old,
he was nearing his end,
when he finally found his adversary.
He was sneaking up now
to the back of the house,
and the man he could see in the conservatory.

This man had a name:
Evil Doctor Strange,
and this 'genius' had made a mistake:
his flower-shop website
had given him away,
even if it was clearly a fake.

Clearly it was part
of a dark master plan,
but the name of the man said it all.
Now Rat Boy was intent
on uncovering the plot,
and causing this Crime Lord's downfall.

He squeezed through a gap
and approaching with stealth,
he got in position to strike.
He breathed deeply in,
preparing to scream
a War Cry with all of his might.

He screamed out his anger,
his vengeance and justice,
he screamed for the humble and poor.
He screamed for the victims
and downtrodden masses,
until he could scream no more!

Evil looked up
from the work he was doing
and beamed a nice welcoming smile.
Slowly he reached
for a sandwich beside him
and pulled something out from inside.

The thing he took out
didn't look like a weapon,
but Rat Boy was really not sure,
his senses went crazy
and blocked out all thought;
he had never smelt Cheddar before.

The curiously named
Evil Doctor Strange
slowly offered the small piece of cheese,
and Rat Boy, conflicted,
was instantly addicted,
and happier than he'd ever been.

In a haze of delight
little Rat Boy died,
and his body soon started to harden.
Evil, in mourning,
took him out in the morning
and buried him at the bottom of the garden.

Dog Boy's Christmas Message

Cats... aren't just for Christmas you know,
they're for games and experiments too.
There really isn't a limit at all
to the wonderful things you can do.

BLEA

A cautionary note though,
before you begin
with test-tubes and rockets and knives,
your Kitten is fragile
with very thin skin,
no padding and only nine lives.

So purchase a facemask and thick rubber gloves
for cleaning up after you've done.
Kitties' intestines are really quite icky,
and picking them up isn't fun.

Woof!

An end.

Lightning Source UK Ltd.
Milton Keynes UK
UKOW06f0018110516

274009UK00001B/9/P

9 781367 727526